f**k it

is the answer

f**k it

is the answer

John C. Parkin & Gaia Pollini

HAY HOUSE

Carlsbad, California • New York City • London • Sydney
Johannesburg • Vancouver • Hong Kong • New Delhi

Copyright © 2014 by John C. Parkin and Gaia Pollini

Published and distributed in the United States by: Hay House, Inc.: www.hayhouse.com® • *Published and distributed in Australia by:* Hay House Australia Pty. Ltd.: www.hayhouse.com.au • *Published and distributed in the United Kingdom by:* Hay House UK, Ltd.: www.hayhouse.co.uk • *Published and distributed in the Republic of South Africa by:* Hay House SA (Pty), Ltd.: www.hayhouse.co.za • *Distributed in Canada by:* Raincoast Books: www.raincoast.com • *Published in India by:* Hay House Publishers India: www.hayhouse.co.in

Cover design: Andrea Amadio • *Interior photos/illustrations:* 229, 231, 233, 240 © Gaia Pollini; 234–35, 238 © Michelangelo Gratton/Getty Images; 236–37 © Shutterstock

All rights reserved. No part of this book may be reproduced by any mechanical, photographic, or electronic process, or in the form of a phonographic recording; nor may it be stored in a retrieval system, transmitted, or otherwise be copied for public or private use—other than for "fair use" as brief quotations embodied in articles and reviews—without prior written permission of the publisher.

The author of this book does not dispense medical advice or prescribe the use of any technique as a form of treatment for physical, emotional, or medical problems without the advice of a physician, either directly or indirectly. The intent of the author is only to offer information of a general nature to help you in your quest for emotional and spiritual well-being. In the event you use any of the information in this book for yourself, the author and the publisher assume no responsibility for your actions.

Library of Congress Control Number: 2014949279

Hardcover ISBN: 978-1-4019-4636-4

10 9 8 7 6 5 4 3 2 1
1st edition, November 2014

Printed in the United States of America

Thanks to Andrea Amadio, designer numero

Introduction

Life can feel like a maze of baffling choices, some small (white wine or red?), some big (this job or that?) – all adding to our stress and worry levels.

Well, F**k It, lighten up – who cares anyway?

Lighten up so much that you start opening this book to help you with your answers.

All these answers have a heavy dose of 'F**k It' injected into them – 'F**k It' being a tried-and-tested route to travel from a tight, uptight, stressed-out kind of life to a more free, open, blissed-out kind of life.

Do you fancy choosing the F**k It Way?

The choice in the end is yours, of course, but if you fancy tasting more freedom in your life, then F**k It may well be your answer.

How to Ask Your Question

DOH! THIS IS THE INTRO –

A general tip is to ask questions that can be answered with a 'yes' or a 'no'. Such as –

'Is this the right time to go travelling?'

Or – 'Should I eat this chocolate cake?'

Or – 'Will I find my true love soon?'

Then, relax… and run your thumb across the pages of the closed book, then open randomly and see what your answer is.

Please don't ask questions that would result in you doing something illegal, or that would harm yourself or others. Or that would be downright stupid.

Don't ask something that could provide an answer that could disturb or upset you or others (e.g. 'Will I survive this journey?').

How to Use the Answers

So you've turned randomly to an answer, and the answer feels right for you. How does that work?

After all, we don't know you. We don't know your situation. (And even if we did, we wouldn't presume to tell you what to do).
And it's not that we are suggesting that answer for you anyway, given that it was your thumb that flicked to that answer.

So how does it work?
Well, the answer you turn to will give you food for thought.
It's likely to set off a thought process that allows you to see your question from different angles, and maybe open up new possibilities for you (like – 'What's below this question?').
In other words, the answer, whichever you turn to, could initiate a psychological

PLEASE TURN AGAIN.

process that assists your decision-making process.
But there's something else to it isn't there? Something less rational.
It's remarkable how often we get, in one form or another, the information we need, when we need it:
Whether it's seeing something on the TV at the right time, or a friend mentioning something or some remarkable coincidence…

There seem to be forces at work out there that none of us fully understand (and we're not going to attempt to provide any answers of that nature here).

This book is another way of tapping into this mysterious realm of interlinked information: a divination tool if you like.

Please use this book as it is intended –
And as the philosophy of F**k It is intended –
LIGHTLY.

This is a lighthearted tool, not a sacred oracle – use all your usual faculties to make any decision.

And obviously, with any decision, as with any act in life, do your utmost not to act in any way that breaks the law, or harms or upsets others, or yourself.

And that includes the questions that you ask (e.g. 'Shall I rob this bank or not?').

DOH! THIS IS THE INTRO –

So, we wouldn't normally suggest this at the beginning of one of our books, but:

It's time to close the book,
Ponder your question,
And turn to your answer.

Enjoy,
John & Gaia x

PLEASE TURN AGAIN.

What's the question beneath

the question you're asking?

F**k It. Stop deliberati

n   g.   Decide now.

Listen to your quietest voice.

③

You need to focus.

④

my friend.

It's time for change

Don't ask.

Just listen.

Say F**k It & do
THE OPPOSITE
of what you think
you should do.

Say F**k It & do
THE OPPOSITE
of what you think
you should do.

GET SOME PERSPECTIVE

and eat it, that's the question.

not what *thinks* right.
Do what *feels* right,

This is coming up because
you haven't learned the lesson yet.
What lesson do you need to learn?

📞 a friend.

... it doesn't matter so much what you decide.

Truth is ...

F**k It. We'll say it.
You're lovely just as you are.
Now what's that question again?

F**k It – toss a

Advice

Accept

17

Make the

Remember that life is short.

most of it.

(18)

Don't be afraid of the easy option.

To: **You**
From: **John & Gaia**
Subject: **The Answer**

The answer is in an email you'll receive today.

Change

nothing.

(21)

Oh yea

n baby

F**k It. Treat it like a

GAME

X not the
MIND

This one
can only be
answered
from the
HEART

Ask your body.

25

You need to be

flexible.

INDULGE YOURSELF

You deserve it.

㉗

Close your eyes
in a moment.
Imagine a stage.
The curtains open.
Your answer appears.

Just stick to what you know is

right.

29

Insert name of others if you prefer –

What would

the Dalai Lama

do?

Don't throw the baby out
with the bathwater

31

Say F**k It eighteen times.
Now what's the answer?

f**k it
f**k it
f**k it
f**k it
f**k it
f**k it
f**k it
f**k it
f**k it
f**k it
f**k it
f**k it
f**k it
f**k it
f**k it
f**k it
f**k it
f**k it
f**k it

It's time to be rational about this.
What are you doing with a book like this?

33

Look at your dreams for guidance.

34

a shit. Please

Give less of

obv

OUS

It is, isn't it?

36

What's the most

it answer to this?

Actually you know the

answer to this very well. You're just resisting it.

Believe

Believe in transformation. Believe in miracles.

what would be
the most healing
answer?

40

F**k It. Put aside your fears. Put aside

your attachments. Is it clearer now?

od for you. Just this process of asking is a good one, ar

od for you. Just this process of asking is a good one, an

Take the boring option.

43

you have all the information you need.

44

F**k It. Just make a decision here. It doesn't

matter so much what you choose, just choose.

In a word,

yes

Fasten your seatbelt.
The answer here is
to take a trip outside
your comfort zone.

47

You're doing good.

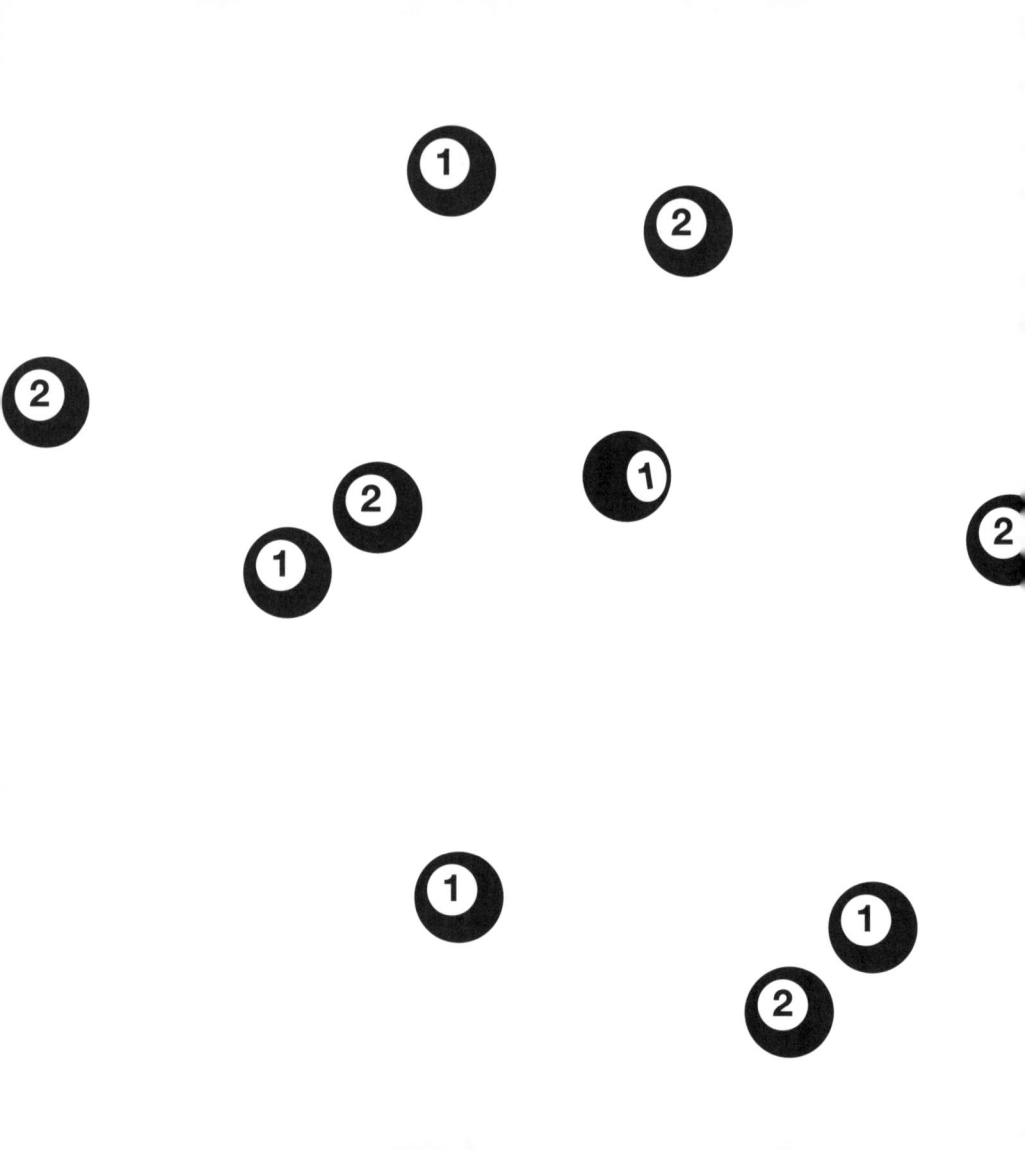

1. Give your options a number ('1' or '2').
2. Close your eyes and point at your answer.

What's the sex

iest way through this one?

50

Go for a walk and mull it over

God talking

nere. Leave it to me.

52

No. 1 Calm down.
No. 2 Turn again.

In a word,

no

Change is the last thing you need at the moment.

55

Take a break.

56

If not now,

when?

THERE ARE NO GUARANTEES.

Bide your time.

59

WATCH C

JT THERE

If you simply trusted that things will work out for the best, what would you do?

61

It's time to

make waves.

Say F**k It and stop
banging
your
head
against
that
wall

63

F**k It. Forget what others will think.

This is for you.

64

F**k It, we'll say it:
don't be a silly bugger.

Do nothing for as long as possible.

66

Z z z z z z z z z

zzzzleep on it.

Well, this is going to be interesting isn't it?

68

Imagine how you'll see this

a year from now.

69

If you're going to repeat a pattern,

make sure it's a positive one.
make sure it's a positive one.
make sure it's a positive one.
make sure it's a positive one.
          it's a positive one.
          it's a positive one.
          it's a positive one.
          it's a positive one.
                 positive one.
                 positive one.
                 positive one.
                 positive one.
                        one.
                        one.

Do you really need our permission?

The answer is staring you right in the face.

72

Not

right now.

73

Say F**k It

and take action.

74

DO YOU REALLY NEED THIS?

75

What was your first thought? Trust that.

76

77

get more information. take time.

78

If you were present now,
embracing reality just as it is,
what would the answer be?

You are not alone.
You are not alone.
You are not alone.
You are not alone.
You are not alone.
You are not alone.
You are not alone.
You are not alone.
You are not alone.

Just remember that.

Hold your horses.

(81)

Who is

your hero?

What would they do?

IF YOU WERE GUARANTEED SUCCESS WHAT WOULD YOU DO?

this page has malfunctioned.
have another go.

Keep moving.

Sometimes you have to do your duty.
Sometimes you have to do your duty.
Sometimes you have to do your duty.
Sometimes you have to do your duty.
Sometimes you have to do your duty.
Sometimes you have to do your duty.
Sometimes you have to do your duty.
Sometimes you have to do your duty.
Sometimes you have to do your duty.
Sometimes you have to do your duty.
Sometimes you have to do your duty.
Sometimes you have to do your duty.
Sometimes you have to do your duty.

Yes, this is your chance.

87

The answer is boring. Sorry.

88

F**k It. Let love guide you here. Pure

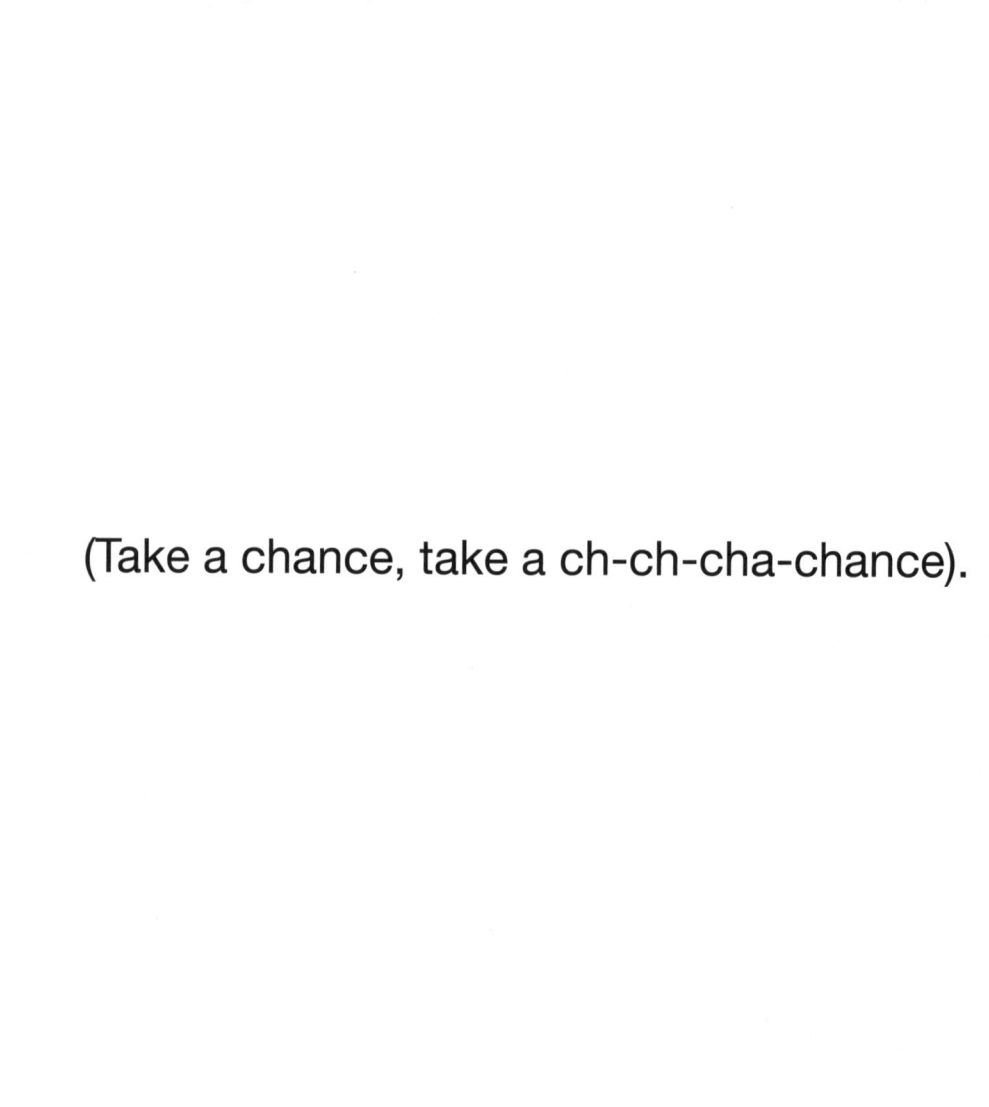

Take a chance on me.

90

Eat some chocolate and things

will become clearer.

Sit back and
let the answer
appear to you.

92

Don't put any more

pressure on yourself.
Say F**k It and sit back.

93

Find a short-cut to

hat you really want.

94

Is there another option here?

Take the simple option.

96

Feel life force pulsing through you.

Now what?

T i   d   y   u   p.

Your answer will come naturally.

One thing we know about this

work won't help.

Mmmm, we're not sure either.

Turn again.

What makes you feel more

relaxed ?

101

Be grateful for what you have,

then choose what you want.

F**k It. Is it really such a big thing?

103

Look at yourself and your choices from the outside; now what?

The answer will become

clear in 48 hours.

Ask a child.

Maybe ~~there~~ is something
you ~~are~~ hiding from yourself ~~here~~?

107

Relax. Mistakes are the g

aps between successes.

Hi,
John & Gaia here.

Now, we know you're not reading this book in a linear front-to-back (or even back-to-front) way, but it's hard not to fall into the traditional convention of saying 'bye' at what feels like the end.

So, even if this is the middle of your experience, as

DOH! THIS IS THE END –

we hope it will be – given that this whole 'F**k It is the Answer' thing could be of service to you for a good long time – we're saying a little *au revoir* here.

And, to mark the occasion, we'd like to offer you something a little special –

We'd like to send you one of these randomly-chosen

F**k It answers by email every day for a month.
Yes, imagine getting an answer in your inbox every day – to help guide you through that day.

To sign up for your free daily answers, just go to –
www.thefuckitlife.com/answers

PLEASE TURN AGAIN.

Well, it's been fun being with you.

Have a good one, or two.
And remember: if in doubt, you know the answer (it has two words).

John & Gaia x

Say F**k It to your plan for today.
Open to something spectacular happening.

THE WAY BOOKS ARE BOUND MEANS THAT THERE ARE OFTEN BLANK PAGES AT THE END. WELL, BLANK PAGES ARE FOR NOTE BOOKS. SO WE'VE SLOTTED IN A FEW EXTRA PAGES OF LOVELINESS FOR YOU – THESE ARE FROM OUR BOOK, *THE WAY OF F**K IT*. AND IF YOU'VE TURNED TO THIS AS AN ANSWER… WELL… IT STILL WORKS. ENJOY, JOHN & GAIA X

You don't have to get it right all the time. F**k It.

THE WAY BOOKS ARE BOUND MEANS THAT THERE ARE OFTEN BLANK PAGES AT THE END. WELL, BLANK PAGES ARE FOR NOTE BOOKS. SO WE'VE SLOTTED IN A FEW EXTRA PAGES OF LOVELINESS FOR YOU — THESE ARE FROM OUR BOOK, *THE WAY OF F**K IT*. AND IF YOU'VE TURNED TO THIS AS AN ANSWER... WELL... IT STILL WORKS. ENJOY, JOHN & GAIA X

F**k It. Do the thing today that most scares you.

THE WAY BOOKS ARE BOUND MEANS THAT THERE ARE OFTEN BLANK PAGES AT THE END. WELL, BLANK PAGES ARE FOR NOTE BOOKS. SO WE'VE SLOTTED IN A FEW EXTRA PAGES OF LOVELINESS FOR YOU – THESE ARE FROM OUR BOOK *THE WAY OF F**K IT*. AND IF YOU'VE TURNED TO THIS AS AN ANSWER... WELL... IT STILL WORKS. ENJOY, JOHN & GAIA X

YOU'VE READ THE BOOK — NOW GO ON A F**K IT RETREAT IN ITALY

This is where it all started: John and Gaia ran their first F**k It Retreat in 2005.
They're now running these famous retreats in spectacular locations around Italy,
including an estate and spa in Urbino, and on the volcano of Stromboli.
Say F**k It and treat yourself to a F**k It Retreat.

*'Anything that helps you let go is okay on a F**k It Retreat.'* THE OBSERVER
*'I witnessed some remarkable transformations during my F**k It Retreat.'* KINDRED SPIRIT

HOW FK IT ARE YOU? TRY OUR QUIZ.**
See how 'F**k It' you really are with the quiz on our site.

WWW.THEFUCKITLIFE.COM/QUIZ

ABOUT THE AUTHORS

John C. Parkin and **Gaia Pollini** said F**k It to their media jobs in London to escape to Italy with their twin boys to set up a retreat centre.

They soon realized that saying 'F**k It' was as powerful as all the Eastern spiritual practices they had been studying for years, and were now teaching at their centre. So they began teaching 'F**k It Retreats'. And they were a hit. The first book *F**k It: The Ultimate Spiritual Way* soon followed and became a bestseller, available in 22 languages.

They have continued to say F**k It over the years – including to running their own retreat centre… they now teach their F**k It Retreats in various spectacular locations around Italy, such as on the volcano of Stromboli (in hotels that other people run).

They spend part of their days spreading the F**k It message – whether on the retreats, or on F**k It eCourses and even with F**k It Music – and the other part watching films with their boys, walking in the hills and napping in the sun.

www.thefuckitlife.com

We hope you enjoyed this Hay House **book. If you'd like to receive our online catalog featuring additional information on Hay House books and products, or if you'd like to find out more about the Hay Foundation, please contact:**

Hay House, Inc., P.O. Box 5100, Carlsbad, CA 92018-5100
(760) 431-7695 or (800) 654-5126
(760) 431-6948 (fax) or (800) 650-5115 (fax)
www.hayhouse.com® • www.hayfoundation.org

* * *

Published and distributed in Australia by: Hay House Australia Pty. Ltd., 18/36 Ralph St., Alexandria NSW 2015 • *Phone: 612-9669-4299 • Fax: 612-9669-4144 • www.hayhouse.com.au*

*Published and distributed in the United Kingdom by: Hay House UK, Ltd.,
Astley House, 33 Notting Hill Gate, London W11 3JQ
Phone: 44-20-3675-2450 • Fax: 44-20-3675-2451 • www.hayhouse.co.uk*

*Published and distributed in the Republic of South Africa by: Hay House SA (Pty), Ltd.,
P.O. Box 990, Witkoppen 2068 • Phone/Fax: 27-11-467-8904 • www.hayhouse.co.za*

Published in India by: Hay House Publishers India, Muskaan Complex, Plot No. 3, B-2, Vasant Kunj, New Delhi 110 070 • Phone: 91-11-4176-1620 • Fax: 91-11-4176-1630 • www.hayhouse.co.in

*Distributed in Canada by: Raincoast Books, 2440 Viking Way, Richmond, B.C. V6V 1N2 •
Phone: 1-800-663-5714 • Fax: 1-800-565-3770 • www.raincoast.com*

* * *

Take Your Soul on a Vacation

Visit www.HealYourLife.com® to regroup, recharge, and reconnect with your own magnificence. Featuring blogs, mind-body-spirit news, and life-changing wisdom from Louise Hay and friends.

Visit www.HealYourLife.com today!

Free e-newsletters from Hay House, the Ultimate Resource for Inspiration

Be the first to know about Hay House's dollar deals, free downloads, special offers, affirmation cards, giveaways, contests, and more!

 Get exclusive excerpts from our latest releases and videos from **Hay House Present Moments**.

 Enjoy uplifting personal stories, how-to articles, and healing advice, along with videos and empowering quotes, within **Heal Your Life**.

 Have an inspirational story to tell and a passion for writing? Sharpen your writing skills with insider tips from **Your Writing Life**.

Sign Up Now!

Get inspired, educate yourself, get a complimentary gift, and share the wisdom!

http://www.hayhouse.com/newsletters.php

Visit www.hayhouse.com to sign up today!

  HealYourLife.com